STEREOTYPICAL LEADERSHIP

LEADERSHIP REPLICATES THE MINDSET OF AN INDIVIDUAL

I0480472

ABHISHEK MISHRA

Contents

Contents

Dedicate

*I want to dedicate this book to all the great leaders who have changed my vision and perspective on Leadership. They inspired me with their characteristics, ethics, and the work they deliver for the betterment of the community. I would like to thank them for not only shaping my mind; they have restructured and shaped my character as a leader. I learned to work and deliver selflessly as being selfless is one of the traits of a successful and great leader. I would like to name those leaders in this book, who has shaped my mind and character as a leader. They all are truly inspiring, and they always offer a lot to society. Those leaders are **Dyana Gladys, Arthi Singh Rathore, Manish Raj, Sabyasachi Mishra, Bansi Rath, Sunil Arunodaya, Kunal Sinha, Ravindra Shahi, Sanjay Teril, Rajan Vashist, Sam Varughese, Saurabh Kulshrestha, Satish Krishnappa, Marc Vanschoenwinkel, Gaurav Dhooper, Kartikeyan Ramamurthy, Harriet Green, and Varun Anand.***

Though I have written this book, this book belongs to all the names I have mentioned here. I have got the idea of writing this book and its content during my association with all of you. It is an honor to work with all these great leaders and learn from them, which is more than any such certification. These leaders taught me the real meaning of "Resilient" & "Perseverance," as these are two key factors to become a successful leader.

Jack Welch once said, "Before you are a leader, success is all about growing yourself. When you become a leader, success is all about growing others". The quality of a successful and great leader is selfless thinking. A person who feels insecure and thinks of themselves can be a good manager but not a leader. So, thanks to all of you for letting me know the actual definition of the word called "selfless." Thank you for teaching, guiding, and directing me in every phase of my life. I owe & dedicate my professional to all of you.

*Lastly would like to thank my wife, **Sailaja Mishra,** who has been a tremendous support to me and who encourage me to write books.*

Introduction

Stereotypical Leadership is not only related to gender stereotyping, but it also includes the thought process of a leader. We are now living in the 21st century, where we witness changes across everywhere. In this vastly changing world, a few people have an old and outdated thought process. In the earlier years, there were leaders, who were having insecurity in sharing knowledge, but it was not their fault; maybe the time and situations allow them to behave accordingly. In the current vastly changing time, will the older thought process be useful? Or will it be dangerous?

This book will demonstrate two types of Stereotypical Leadership. One is a Stereotypical mindset, and another one is a gender stereotype. Both can be equally dangerous and can have a severe impact on society.
In all the circumstances, you can perceive how the equivalent supportive individuals surrounding them can meet with either resistance or gratitude.

The great leader sees the glass half full that everybody needs to support them. In the interim, the Stereotypical leader is worried and cannot make sense of why everything is generally so disappointing and trying to give them more work.

After reading my book, it is easy to say, "I will follow all these and will become a good leader," but it is always harder at the moment.

You must have a positive & growth mindset, manage external pressure, and fight with your imposter syndrome that has crawled into your mind most of the time.

Leadership is not something that comes naturally to most people. The key is to stay positive remain clam even when you slip, and even when you face challenges. Teams respect such leaders who always admit their mistakes and put in the work to make it right. The payoff is well worth your investment: loyalty, hard work, and seeing the best work from your team.

In this book, I have explained how good/ genuine leaders looks like and the trait and characteristics of a great & successful leader, what is Stereotypical Leadership means and how it originated, types of Stereotypical Leadership, and a comparison between a Stereotypical leader vs. good leader. The book will help all of us understanding Stereotypical Leadership in detail and how it can have a severe impact on our society.

I welcome each one of you to join the journey of understanding Stereotypical Leadership and its various aspects. I hope we all will have a thrilling and meaningful adventure together.

Chapter-1

Leadership Meaning, Factors and Characteristics

To understand Stereotypical Leadership, first, let's know the leadership meaning, it's factors and characteristics. I have explained it here in the 1st Chapter.

Objectives

Readers will able to understand the followings:

- Understand the concept of Leadership
- Define Leadership
- Comprehend the factors of Leadership
- Explain the attributes of an effective leader

Meaning

Leadership is an energizing factor that accelerates the functioning of an organization. A great leader can inspire the entire community through his thoughts and deeds. These influences radiate and energize his community towards a common goal. Successful implementation of the programs and projects of every institution/company relies upon the leadership behavior and administrators of concerned institutions.

Leadership-Meaning

According to Warren Bennis and Bert Nanus' article in 1985 on leadership, "Leadership seems to be the marshaling of abilities processed by way of a majority however utilized by a minority. But it is something that may be found out through anyone, taught to everyone, denied to no one".

Leadership is a process through which a person affects others to perform an objective and directs the organization in a way that makes it extra cohesive and coherent.

A leader is a person who helps others to attain goals. The more the quantity of followers suggests the intensity of influencing the strength of the leader, and the extraordinary success the attainment of worthy goals, the more obvious the Leadership. Outstanding leaders combine precise strategic materials and robust interpersonal procedures to formulate and implement techniques that produce effects and sustainable competitive advantage.

It takes a lot of dedication and practice to become a good leader; they are not born. If one has the preference and willpower, he can grow to be a powerful chief. Good leaders develop via a never-ending system of self-study, education, training, and experience (Jago, 1982). Developing group spirit among subordinates and provoking them to reap targeted desires are the warranted characteristics of an effective leader.

A good leader can build those professional skills through non-stop works and effective schooling programs.

Leadership-Definition

Here are the definitions of Leadership by experts, and the definition stands the same since 1950.

According to Stogdill (1950), Leadership definition is "Considers management is the method of influencing the activities of an organized group in its efforts closer to goal putting and goal attainment."

According to Tannenbaum (1961), leadership definition is "Leadership is interpersonal effect exercised in a scenario and directed through verbal exchange method, closer to the attainment of a specified purpose or goals."

According to Terry (1988), leadership definition is "Leadership is largely a continuous system of influencing behavior. A leader breathes lifestyles into the group and motivates it in the direction of goals. The lukewarm desires for achievement are converted right into a burning ardor for accomplishment".

According to Key and Case (1990), leadership definition is "Leadership is the procedure of influencing and helping others to paintings enthusiastically toward achieving objectives."

Factors of Leadership

There are four significant factors in Leadership, such as Leader, Followers, Communication, and Situation. A leader has to have a genuine understanding of who they are, what they know, and what they can do. It is the followers, now not the leader or someone else who determines whether or not the leader is successful. If they do not believe or lack self-belief of their chief, then they will be uninspired. To be successful, one has to convince his fans, not himself or his superiors, that he is worthy of being followed.

Followers are the subordinates of the head. Leaders need to know their people. The fundamental start point is having a good understanding of human nature, including needs, emotions, and motivation. Leaders ought to come to recognize their employees be, know, and do attributes. Communication maintains desirable courting between leader and followers as nicely as shows the leader's efficiency.

A leader leads through two-way communication. Much of it is nonverbal. Dialogue should be well mannered and gentle in manner. It must improve human relations. There are many different conditions one leader must face. What the Leader does in one situation will now not continually work in another.

A leader must use their judgment to determine the first-rate direction of motion and the leadership style wanted for every scenario. For example, leaders may need to confront an employee for beside the point behavior, and however, if the war of words is too past due or too early, too harsh or too weak, then the consequences may also prove ineffective. The situation generally has a more significant effect on a leader's motion than his or her traits. It is because even as attributes may have an excellent balance over a length of time, they've little consistency across situations (Mischel, 1968).

Various forces will affect these four factors. Examples of compulsions are relationship with seniors, the talent of followers, the informal leaders within the enterprise, and the way the employers organized themselves.

Characteristics of a Leader

Distinct humans will have unique thoughts of what a notable leader is. There is no unmarried mildew to craft a pacesetter, but management is available in all sizes and styles.

Even as incredible leaders can be determined in some of the industries and walk their specific trips to the pinnacle, there are definite trends and characteristics those incredible women and men often percentage. Whether you analyze leaders or ask people immediately, the under a set of features and abilities gets the point out.

The Characteristics of a Great Leader

A great leader is not just an individual; it's a character. Character and personality define a great leader, and consciousness plays a more prominent role in determining an individual's style and personality. The following characteristics will define the character and personality of a great leader, and it will assist you to speak your Leadership imaginative and prescient to others.

1. *A positive attitude:* Management without a positive mindset is alternatively hard to achieve. Who would like to observe a pacesetter who always seems pessimistic or irritated? A remarkable leader knows Leadership is ready main with example. If you can stay advantageous in the face of difficulties and you may method demanding situations with a grin for your face, you set an example for subordinates.

   Excellent leaders have executed their homework in terms of the science of exceptional thinking. A great mindset is not just about keeping the mood upbeat within the crew – it may provide higher outcomes for the team in terms of productiveness and innovation. A famous example of this comes within the form of a candle look at, which researchers have used to study advantageous feelings.

Dan red, author of whole New thoughts and pressure, has written approximately the experiment. The experiment asks the participants to connect a candle to the wall without the wax dripping at the table. Dan handed over a matchbook, a candle, and a container of thumbtacks to use during the experiment. Quiet, the more rewards the individuals supplied, the slower they are at solving the problem. The test highlights, in step with pink, the essence of excellent wondering in place of rewards and punishment because of the center of Leadership. Why does a beautiful mindset have such a significant impact on performance?

"high-quality feelings flood our brains with dopamine and serotonin, chemical substances that not best make us experience right, but dial up the learning centers of our brains to better tiers. They assist us in organizing new statistics, hold that information within the brain longer, and retrieve it faster in a while."

A practical mindset does not mean the leader is ignorant of problems or suffering. It requires the technique for solving issues and completing tasks to be positive in preference to a terrible one. In the choice of thinking about the drawback of the work in advance, the leader wants to respect the most refreshing aspects.

2. *A focused approach:* Leadership offers with the implementation of a specific vision. It indicates that a splendid leader can live centered and make sure the group works correctly in the direction of accomplishing the goals. A pacesetter is a person that will manual the manner, and if the leader is ignorant of in which he or she is going, the team will quickly locate someone else to follow. A focused approach does not just suggest staying in contact with the right here and now. Although the leader must be continually on the pinnacle of what is going on, it's crucial to look beforehand as correctly.

To hold cognizance, the leaders must have a course of action, which has details for overcoming distinctive barriers the world ought to throw within the way. A targeted method is mostly about having a robust leadership method and framework.

Maintaining focus may be difficult in today's world. It's crucial to prepare yourself for the tasks in advance and improve your reaction to existence's little activities through obtaining extra information. The more you understand about management, your organization, the human mind, the easier it could be to react and prepare. Moreover, you furthermore may want to ensure the vision is genuinely recognized.

It's hard to live targeted on the direction if you aren't entirely satisfied where you are walking. In an extra sensible level, you ought to additionally watch the under video via Actualized.org. It offers top-notch guidelines in a way to be a more significant effect on everything you do.

3. *A decisive mind:* Leaders need to make choices. In case you aren't capable of determine among Plan A and Plan B inside a fixed timeframe, you're most probably doing something incorrectly: either you don't have the understanding to be a frontrunner; otherwise, you aren't decisive enough to make a stand. Nobody has said management is straightforward.

Decision-making matters since leaders do not regularly have the luxury of time. The global business movements rapid, and the leader needs to be always prepared to make a call on wherein to head next. The project is steeper as a pacesetter cannot merely decide; however, they need to make specific the choice is the ideal one and advantages the crew. The way to be better at making decisions. Lisa Nalbone has recommended a top-notch model for selection- making:

The above manual allows you to at work and in private existence. It is essential to understand the 'why,' explore the exceptional possibilities instead of merely sticking on your first idea, and paste on your decision after you've made it. Subsequently, regardless of how big or small the decision is, attempt evaluating it afterward to understand how powerful your choice became in reaching what you desired it to achieve.

4. *An empowering character:* A leader is often known as desirable as the human beings around her or him. Even though management can suggest the shape of energy is more hierarchical than equal, it does not indicate the leader is the best man or woman to get things accomplished. Leadership is often about developing other human beings' competencies in preference to appearing responsibilities as the leader.

When the leader's awareness of empowering and nurturing skills round them, they ensure the team achieves its goals quicker. But empowerment is essential beyond the realistic factor of coaching human beings' new abilities.

Recognizing other human beings' skills will have a massive motivational factor. In case you assist someone ends up better, you offer them with new opportunities and new challenges – all of which can make the person happier and extra inspired every. You confront a keen team member, one who desires to spend time experimenting and studying, rather than doing the identical things time and again.

5. *A communicative ability:* The capability to speak might be the feature; most people associate with appropriate leaders. Leaders need to communicate the imaginative and prescient clearly with a purpose to reap following and motivating others in the back of their motive. Yet, conversation and all that it entails is frequently alternatively misunderstood as a concept. It is not honest about the ability to explain matters to different humans, but also about the capacity to read other humans and to concentrate on what people around you're announcing.

A first communique constructed around the subsequent constructing blocks:

The capacity to listen – This includes know-how non-verbal cues but also being capable of use mirrored image and clarification on your advantage.

The capacity to sympathize and to empathize – You want to have the capability to recognize different people's emotions. For a leader, it is critical to be aware of what goes on within the lives of the subordinates so that it will better reflect their feelings.

The capability to encourage – during any kind of communique part of the point of interest must be on encouragement. It can suggest praising the person's efforts, making them feel welcome, or permitting them to sense like their reviews are valued. Motivation is mostly the ability to have interaction; to ensure the discussion isn't just one-sided.

Moreover, while you are communicating with a person, you want to first clarify your message to yourself. Always make sure you are aware of the center message you want the man or woman to get from your dialogue because this alone can upload much readability to the talk.

6. *An empathetic nature:* The exploded view of a leader frequently painted an alternatively darkish picture of the leader. Leaders considered dictators who do not care about their team members. However, they pursue the objectives, no matter the results.

Yet, the global has modified, and people now understand how essential 'softer' values are in terms of success management. Empathy and the capability to do not forget other people, at the same time as pursuing the imaginative and prescient, are a part of the leader's schedule.

Leigh Buchanan's article in Inc. highlights the significance of empathy, now not merely in terms of innovation, but also for business sustainability. Compassion and an actual problem for different humans are not best a sturdy motivational tool for purchasing matters achieved. Still, it also enables leaders to better put in force their imaginative and prescient. The potential to recognize what other people are going thru enables decision-making.

Chapter-2

The 27 Qualities and Traits of a Successful Leader

As we have understood the leadership meaning, its factor, and characteristics, so now it would be essential to understand the qualities and traits of a leader, which will make them a great leader or a successful leader. Let's follow those traits and characteristics. I have mentioned 27 such qualities and attributes in this chapter, and those based on my research about leadership attributes

Several leadership developments nearly come within ourselves. Those are the characteristics that might be tougher to teach, however, which makes the leader as successful and a great leader.

Successful leaders are the electricity and use their mind at the back of their businesses. They are the visionaries charged with steering their logo around pitfalls. They ought to know when to capture possibilities and the way to rally employees to work difficult toward their enterprise's goals.

Influential leaders transcend the identity of "manager" or "boss." they have determined a way to achieve the proper mixture of air of secrecy, enthusiasm, and self-assurance, probably with a healthy dose of success and timing. It can appear like some human beings are merely proficient with these capabilities, but the truth is that maximum leadership traits can be discovered and sharpened with time and exercise. You can start constructing your achievement by using the mentioned 27 qualities or characteristics, which will have the tendencies of a powerful and successful leader.

1. **Committed:** A fantastic leader must show dedication. Pleasurable your imaginative and prescient gained to happen in a single day, and you want on the way to convince all and sundry else that you received to disappear while things get hard. If you make a promise, you need to preserve it. You may not merely hold forth about accomplishing A, B, and C, however, you want to show that you are certainly going to do it.

Dedication matters for two motives. First, when you show dedication, you assist build belief. The team and all and sundry worried about the challenge could be able to consider your phrase. Accept as real with will maintain work morale up and assist you in attaining targets quicker since people do not need to second-guess what your objectives are.

However, the second component of commitment is to set an example. As noted throughout the article, Leadership is ready to place an instance, and if you show dedication to your phrase, your subordinates may be inspired to stick to their promises. The usage of your example of intricate paintings, you will make sure the human beings around you feel influenced to do the same thing.

2. **Passionate:** Passion must be on the heart of the entirety you do. It does not matter whether you are a leader of a multi-billion company or a lumberjack; without ardor, you would not achieve success. You can understand its significance when you view it because of the fuel for your truck. In case you do not have enough gasoline, i.e., ardor, you will finally run out of steam, and your journey might end quickly. But in case you are passionate about keeping the ball rolling and ensure your team member that you have enough fuel, you can keep riding.

Furthermore, passion facilitates in management because it could encourage different human beings. Consider someone is doing a task certainly for the sake of doing it. They might show up each morning and finish the tasks as informed. However, there is no burn inside them.

Then again, you have got a person who is continually excited to begin a task, who talks approximately the jobs and springs up with new thoughts and guidelines.

Which one would you sense extra relaxed following?

Passion can, of the route, appear depleted at times. Much like including gasoline in your car, you want to now and again re-light your ardor. The foundation advised those six approaches to locate your enthusiasm.

Undertake the proper method of looking for ardor – Do not assume locating your passion can be not possible but be inspired by way of the opportunities you have got in front of you.

Become aware of your' peak moments' – examine your studies and locate the moments that stand out.

Find the connection – Your passions would possibly every so often seem distinct from every different; however, try to discover the connections linking your pastimes collectively. You certainly need to find a proper angle for your ardor. At the same time, as you should not ever do something for the sake of being profitable, you do want to make sure your passion can preserve the kind of way of life you need.

Do not be fearful of the resistance – Your internal voice will try to come up with all types of reasons you should not observe your heart. Resist the fear. Explore your comfort zone – ardor calls for you to take the plunge and to step out of doors of the comfort quarter.

3. *Honest:* Another trait which leaders need to have is honesty. An influential leader can deal with people with recognition and care while staying accurate. Leadership is not about wiping matters underneath the carpet. If there is a hassle, a high-quality leader can discover it, speak about it, and find solutions to it. A frontrunner does not upload a sugar coating on matters; however, they use their conversation abilities to ensure humans are aware of the problems.

Honesty additionally means openness approximately the tactics and the implementation of the imaginative and prescient. The leader must usually be as informative and open about the tasks ahead as feasible with the subordinates.

The more critical information the subordinates have, the better they can conduct their work as properly. If the vision and the goals are shrouded in thriller, it can be difficult for the subordinates to commit to the process thoroughly.

4. *Confident:* A brilliant leader is always assured. If they are hesitant or appear to have a loss of belief in their very own abilities, Team members would not sense at ease following their lead. Good leaders never have a second thought on their level of confidence. However, they are always aware of their strengths and know the way to use them to get maximum results.

While things are going wrong, human beings often begin searching round them for consolation and help. A pacesetter is a person who sticks out in those times because they display composure that relaxes other people. If a ship is sinking, you observe the captain, and you need him to give you orders lightly on what to do, no longer run around yelling, "we'll all die."

The key to recognize and excel in confidence is the realization that it does not imply self-delight or arrogance. The capacity to realize you can attain your dreams does not suggest the same as questioning you are the best person who can finish the job.

There several ways to gain confidence. First, you need to learn how to understand yourself and your abilities. It is necessary to analyze and gets ahead of your strengths and weaknesses as someone, a leader, and a worker.

You also need to keep studying extra about the world around you. The capacity to research new matters, as well as the braveness to strive things you've never executed earlier than are crucial for enhancing and growing your confidence.

5. **_Accountable:_** Trust requires accountability. You could not begin trusting a leader or experience comfortable with the method if you do not treat your team member equally. To developing a team, most publications point responsibility as the cornerstone of getting matters to work. In terms of management, accountability is regularly now, not just in terms of the chief's very own errors. However, a fantastic leader takes duty for all people's performance.

It can seem brutal; however, a splendid chief is aware that ultimately the buck stops with them. While people usually need to take duty within a team, it's far the chief's role to ensure things won't pass wrong. One of the most important reasons at the back of the lack of consideration in nowadays, CEOs frequently comes precisely from the reality that leaders are not showing sufficient accountability.

At some point in the financial crash, the public witnessed some of the leaders either avoiding the consequences or on step away with a hefty severance package deal. In case you want to build trust, then you have to show guts to accept the mistake, which is done by your team and the broader community as a pacesetter, you need to show duty.

6. *Inspirational:* In case you put all the above collectively, an image of an inspirational chief will emerge. In any case, one of the key characteristics that separate the leader from the rest is the capacity to inspire. A frontrunner is someone who can outline his or her vision and right away capture the imagination of other humans. You will not observe someone that does not spark an emotion in you, who does not make you feel better, and who does not convince you of the path they are heading. You observe someone who will make you experience enthusiastic about the journey ahead.

An inspirational Leader is not always just capable of communicating effectively; they also can assist the people around them to obtain the imaginative and prescient. Therefore, inspirational is not the best sincerely approximately the potential to 'candy speak.'

The proper concept is to show others how something can be accomplished and supplying people with the tools to trade matters into something unique. As a leader, you want an excellent way to encourage humans to dream but to act in line with one's goals additionally.

Careers educate Kathy Caprino wrote in Forbes approximately the three center elements defining inspirational people. Inline with Caprino, inspirational humans have:

They created their direction in preference to following what different human beings are doing. They are additionally engrossed in their passion, frame, and soul.

- They raised to become interested in different humans in preference to centering themselves in the middle of the entirety they do. Proposal people want to help and empower others as it gives them with achievement and pleasure.
- Happen to be fantastic at telling tales by the usage of new perspectives and adding their very own experiences to the entirety they do.

The above tendencies and traits are on the coronary heart of superb leaders. The features are often innate, but it does not suggest they cannot or should not learn and developed similarly.

An excellent leader recognizes the significance of these developments and is aware that all and sundry can use them in their quest to become a fantastic leader.

7. *Self-Managing:* It is laborious to manage others effectively if you cannot manage yourself. Self-managing suggests that having the ability to place your goals and being chargeable for accomplishing those objectives. As a good leader, you need to be able to regulate some time, attention, and emotions, whereas remaining alert to your strengths, weaknesses, and potential sources of bias.

Exceptional leaders always show their excellent quality of handling stress and reconciliation in their personal and skilled lives. However, you need to bear in mind conjointly the importance of compassion Associate in learning be able to reply to individuals and events in an acceptable approach. Bear in mind to keep up self-control and discipline in your actions, though' you ought to avoid changing into a fault reserved or inflexible.

8. *Acting Strategically:* A forward-wondering, open-minded approach is essential for today's leaders. Inline with a Harvard business Publishing report: "crucial abilities for a leader is to think & act strategically, and leaders should alter their techniques in such a way-

where they can gain opportunities, they need to think strategically to tackle extraordinary challenges continually." Wondering how to act strategically and how to make it an ongoing process that entails assessing your organizational environments. You could domesticate strategic questioning using:

- Being curious and interested in your company and the broader enterprise environment.
- Being flexible to your attitude and trying new procedures and thoughts.
- Focusing on the future and considering your company's operational conditions and keeping a fantastic outlook.

9. ***Being an Effective Communicator:*** Powerful leaders know while to talk and when to listen. They may be persuasive communicators and are capable of directly and succinctly explain their employees the whole lot from organizational desires to unique responsibilities. If people don't understand or aren't privy to your expectations, they may fall short, so the extra unique you may be, the higher.

You need that allows you to speak on all tiers: one on one, to the branch and the whole personnel, in addition to thru smartphone, email, and social media.

Communication built on a constant waft of verbal and nonverbal exchanges of thoughts and statistics so works on being approachable and involving human beings from specific ranges.

10. ***Being Accountable and Responsible:*** Successful managers recognize the way to use power and authority correctly without overwhelming or overpowering personnel. Influential leaders maintain themselves responsible and take obligation for their errors—and that they expect others to do the equal. They can work inside installed approaches and be productive and green of their selections.

They recognize the importance of supporting and inspiring individuality at the same time as also understanding organizational systems and the want to observe guidelines and policies. They may be able to stability different perspectives while taking appropriate motion.

Setting Clear Goals and Persisting in Achieving Them.

Here is a boiled-down version for obtaining air of secrecy: Set clean desires and be determined and practical in achieving them. Again, all of it up with unshakable self-confidence.

In case you radiate enthusiasm and are enthusiastic about what you are doing, people might get attracted to you.

Remember the fact that writing your goals down is fundamental to the achievement of each you and your organization. But engaging in those desires takes time. In case you give up, so will all and assorted around you. To be an exceptional leader, you ought to be willing to maintain going when others tempted to throw the towel within.

11. ***Having A Vision for The Future:*** Exceptional leaders can investigate their company's future and make precise, concrete desires to benefit their business enterprise. They may be assured and optimistic, inspiring enthusiasm in the ones around them. Being a visionary is set handling alternate at the same time as putting a balance among balance and growth. You must comprise new processes without getting distracted from the primary goals.

Being visionary approach expertise that continuous trade is going on all around you, so what worked for you in the past might not always work. Exercise being adaptable and agile as you put in force new strategies and permit your organization model to adapt over time.

12. ***Managing Complexity:*** Leaders ought to be trouble solvers who can make selections under hastily moving instances. Mastering to lead in a complicated environment is a crucial ability for any leader. Even earlier than any definitive data is to had; effective leaders ought to examine a situation's complexity and pick appropriate courses of movement. Being capable of scan the surroundings on the lookout for diffused tendencies and signs of disruptive alternate and set up practices that allow your organization to reply unexpectedly.

13. ***Fostering Creativity and Innovation:*** Leaders must have the courage to risk experimentation and encourage creativity. Doing this can promote the innovation to steer your company to new locations and around the twists and turns of a changing commercial enterprise panorama.

The secret is to continually be persistent in pursuing your goals, and open-minded and flexible in how you get there. Inspire the human beings around you to spend at least 15 percent of their time exploring new ideas through brainstorming and prototyping.

14. *Creating Lasting Relationships:* Compelling leaders do more than simply inspire others to observe them; they recognize how to encourage their employees to attempt wholeheartedly for his or her business enterprise's dreams. Employees who sense valued and appreciated, who sense like what they do makes a distinction, will sense invigorated to push more challenging to acquire fulfillment for his or her organization.

Good leaders additionally consider that they want to be dominant at networking, no longer just to strengthen their careers, but for the benefit in their corporation. By growing a considerable and sundry community of humans, leaders establish impactful relationships with clients, clients, partners, and even competitors.

15. *Learning Agility:* Top-notch leaders recognize that the strength in their management is built on their potential to evolve to unexpectedly converting circumstances and to know how and while to capture on opportunities amid a converting panorama.

Having an unquenchable curiosity will fuel your preference to learn and grow continuously.

Mastering agility hinges on developing critical questioning abilities, being accepting of uncertainty, having social and emotional intelligence, and continually having the preference and resolution to push forward.

16. *Integrity:* The significance of integrity must be evident. Even though it could no longer necessarily be a metric in worker evaluations, honesty is essential for the individual and the company. It is vital for pinnacle-stage executives who are charting the organization's route and making infinite different massive decisions. Our studies display that integrity may additionally, in reality, be a capability blind spot for companies. Make sure your organization reinforces the significance of integrity to leaders at diverse ranges.

17. *Ability to Delegate:* Delegating is one of the core responsibilities of a leader. However, it could be complex to delegate effectively. The aim is not merely to lose yourself up — it's additionally to allow your direct reviews, facilitate teamwork, offer autonomy, cause higher decision-making, and assist your candid reviews in developing. That will enable you to delegate well. You also want to assemble with your team to ensure they agree with your delegation plan.

18. *Self-Awareness:* At the same time, as that is a more significant inwardly targeted talent, self-attention is paramount for Leadership. The higher you understand yourself, the greater effective you can be. Do you know how different human beings view you, or the way you display up at paintings? Try to find out about the four elements of self-cognizance, and the way you may dig into everything.

19. *Gratitude:* Giving thanks can cause you to a much better leader. The feeling will cause higher vanity, reduced depression and anxiety, and even higher sleep. Few folks often say "thank you" at work, also though most of the people say they would be willing to figure more durable for AN appreciative boss. Follow the following pointers for giving thanks and additional active feeling.

20. *Influence:* For some human beings, "affect" seems like a dirty phrase. However, being able to convince human beings through logical, emotional, or cooperative appeals is a component of being an inspiring, powerful chief. The impact is quite distinct from manipulation, and it wishes authenticity and transparency. It requires emotional intelligence and accepts as true with-building. Here are four keys to influencing others.

- *Organizational Intelligence:* They apprehend a way to get things completed and embrace the fact of working within organizational politics to transport teams and important projects ahead.

- *Team promotion:* Leaders cut thru the noise to promote themselves authentically however credibly — even as additionally selling what is precise for the whole organization

- *Trust Building:* since management regularly includes guiding human beings via threat and exchange, agree with is vital.

- *Leveraging Networks:* No chief is an island. They may empower through their connections with others.

21. *Empathy:* Empathy correlated with job overall performance. If you display understanding closer to your direct reviews, our research shows you are much more likely to be regarded as a better performer with the aid of your boss. Empathy may found out, and further to make you more productive, it is going to improve, give you the results you want to add, and people around you. Organizations can follow these five steps to encourage empathy at work.

- ***Talk about empathy:*** let managers understand that empathy topics. Many managers consider assignment-orienting abilities inclusive of tracking and planning to be extra essential to controlling the performance of their team members. Studies show that information, worrying, and growing others is simply as crucial. If not greater vital, especially in these days' body of employees, explain that giving time and interest to others encourages empathy, which in flip enhances your overall performance and improves your perceived effectiveness.

- ***Teach listening skills:*** To understand others and feel what they are feeling, managers must be a good listener. Professional listeners let others know that they are getting attention and that they explicit know-how of worries and issues. When a supervisor is a great listener, humans sense respected and accept as real with can develop. Managers have the cognizance of paying attention to hear the that means behind what others are saying via taking note of not most straightforward the words said, but nonverbal cues such as tone, tempo of speech, facial expressions, and gestures.

- *Encourage good perspective-taking:* Managers should always place themselves in a different man or woman's vicinity. For managers, this consists of deliberating the personal experience or angle in their personnel. It also can be implemented for fixing troubles, dealing with conflicting, or riding innovation.

- *Cultivate compassion:* Guide managers who care approximately how a person else feels or recall the outcomes that business selections have on employees, customers, and groups. Pass past the standard-trouble values statement and permit time for compassionate reflection and reaction.

- *Support global managers*: The ability to be empathetic is especially critical for leaders operating in global corporations or across cultural boundaries. Running across cultures calls for managers to apprehend human beings who've quite different views and reports. Empathy generates a hobby in and appreciation for others, paving the way to more productive running relationships. As managers hone their empathy capabilities, they enhance their management effectiveness and growth their probabilities of fulfillment within the task.

Empathetic leaders are belongings to organizations, in element, because they can correctly construct and hold relationships — a critical a part of main groups anywhere within the world.

22. *Courage:* It can be tough to speak up at work, whether you need to voice a brand-new idea, provide comments to an instantaneous document, or flag a concern for a person above you. That is part of the reason courage is a crucial skill for appropriate leaders. In place of averting problems or allowing conflicts to fester, braveness will enable leaders to step up and flow things inside the right direction.

23. *Respect:* Treating people with recognition on an everyday foundation is one of the most critical things a pacesetter can do. It will ease tensions and war, create acceptance as accurate with, and improve effectiveness. Recognize is higher than the absence of disrespect, and it may show in lots of unique methods.

24. *Resilience:* While the going gets tough, the tough get going. You might have heard this adage many times, but did you realize that brilliant leaders additionally comply with this rule. They are resilient and feature a practical mindset.

No matter how severe the instances is probably, you may discover them rallying their followers. While the majority are busy complaining approximately the troubles, notable leaders usually recognition on answers, now not the Problems.

25. *Emotional Intelligence:* Correct leaders always have a better effect; however, how do they increase their impact at the factor wherein people receive what they say. They do that by connecting with human beings emotionally. That's when emotional intelligence comes into play.

Here are several motives why a frontrunner should be emotionally intelligent.
- Manipulate emotions successfully
- Better social recognition
- Seamless communications
- Struggle decision

With emotional intelligence, leaders can manage their feelings, which prevents negative emotions from influencing their choice-making abilities. As a result, they are much less likely to make hasty selections. Moreover, emotionally smart leaders are top-notch at the knowledge of the feelings and care approximately the emotions of others.

That is not all; leaders who have got this administration high-quality no longer only handle warfare in a better manner; however, they additionally play a critical role in war resolution.

26. *Transparency:* One of the first-class ways to win the belief of your teams is through being transparent. in place of hiding records, you must openly proportion it with them. By way of giving visibility in your followers, they will buy into your vision and support you with conviction in attaining the aim. Greater importantly, it gives your followers clarity, autonomy and causes them to experience more empowered while maintaining them engaged.

27. *Vision and Purpose:* "Good business leaders create a vision, articulate the vision, passionately own the vision, and relentlessly drive it to completion."—Jack Welch

Good leaders continuously have imaginative and perceptive and reason. They, not the handiest, visualize the future themselves but also proportion their vision with their team. While their team members could see the large picture, they can see in which they may be heading. A brilliant leader is going above and beyond. Explains why they are transferring? And at the same time, they ensure their team is moving and shares the approach and action plan to achieve that goal.

Chapter-3

What is Stereotypical Leadership? How it originated & 6 ways to reduce Stereotype

Now, as we have understood the Leadership meaning, its factors, characteristics, and traits to become a good or successful leader, so, it will be easy to understand the stereotypical Leadership. Here I present the definition of stereotypical Leadership, its origination, and how we can reduce stereotypes.

Stereotypical Leadership

Stereotyping in Leadership means making decisions relating to people supported merely some attributes or one attribute associated with a demographic cluster. Which might be race, religion, ethnicity, temperament, generation, or any vary of broad categorical groups one may even be a member.

The reason to avoid this may be twofold: you will likely err because of stereotypes fail to predict in day-to-day contexts, and those who are stereotyped will know they are stereotyped. Avoiding stereotyping due to the previous reason needs to be a no brainer – smart leaders regularly ought to kind the only decisions.

The second reason, however, is insidious because it will artificially limit your human resources, modification of the culture of your workplace in a negative way, and you may not even bear in mind until the damage happens. When it comes to how we determine others, not exclusively tend to determine what we expect to resolve, but meeting wired expectations.

How and from where Stereotypical Leadership originated

We are excellent at detecting when we tend to determine the target of stereotyping. Whether the stereotype is positive or negative, most of us feel uncomfortable when being stereotyped – if something, it encroaches on one's individuality.

This ability to identify stereotyping is a component of a group of social functions that persist from our necessary instincts from thousands of years ago. Those who were lacking such occasions throughout those periods may not have a chance to live long enough to procreate.

What this means is that nearly all people have inherited this social nature, which is profoundly primal and necessary. Our social life can be incompatible with civil society because the world is vastly changing today, and it is the culprit behind the foremost elusive social problems. What this means is when we tend to sight being a target of stereotyping, which is very demotivating.

The flip side of this issue is our effort to labeled. Once it involves people, at the very minimum, we have got a tendency to tagged people as friends and foes. Overall, we follow the steps of others in the world to become part of social and cultural life. In this process, knowingly or unknowingly, we stereotype people, which may be the reason why we have stereotyped others. It is a basic human phenomenon, and we would do well as leaders to understand and overcome it in ourselves.

Good leaders regularly strive to understand themselves and others – and understanding individuals rather than groups serve to dilute our need to be compelled to stereotype. Even good intentions tend to possess dangerous outcomes once it involves stereotyping.

Possible ways to reduce stereotype

Now that I have explained Stereotypes, it's meaning and its qualities. Now let us understand how we can reduce the tendency of stereotype. There are six possible ways of lowering the possibilities of stereotype, and those are the followings:

i.	*Accept & Decide*
ii.	*Have Courage*
iii.	*Catch Yourself*
iv.	*Reprogram Yourself*
v.	*Practice*
vi.	*Have Patience, Persevere*

To have a better understanding, here are the detailed explanations for each of these six ways mentioned here.

i.   *Accept & Decide:* Accept that we are human, and, as a human, it's obvious to have some tendency to stereotype. Just because we think and believe that stereotype does not make it real. Even though we believe that we are a fair and truthful leader, but in reality, we may be more biased than we think. We all are human, and stereotyping is a normal human tendency. We will have to admit this, and we all must strive to avoid it. Accepting that we may need to change is the first step and the most critical and essential step. Then decide you will attempt to change.

ii.   *Have Courage:* Any changes that we all go through is always required lots of guts and courage. Have the courage to admit that you are wrong, even though you cannot save anything. Being honest is a great thing and being honest first and foremost with yourself and then extend honesty to others in every and every social context that you engage yourself. We all tend to develop a pattern of social behaviors or a persona that can get in the way of change. We would wish to find once our social identity conflicts with our fairness and honesty.

iii. ***Catch Yourself:*** Accepting, deciding, and having courage is significant. However, it may not be enough. You will need to build skills to help you change. Which implies you will need to learn to catch yourself. Having a family member, colleague, or friend partner with you will help you to kickstart this. As an example, create an agreement that each of you will commit to catch and notify each other when making stereotyping comments, which could help you to build the skills of real-time self-introspection – finding yourself at the moment.

iv. ***Reprogram Yourself:*** One of the best ways is to reprogram yourself; So the tendency of understanding a person as only an individual does not rule you. Understanding others and empathizing could also be a big part of this. Look at everyone and understand their nature. Try to study what is necessary to them, the things they need to try to, and what their lives are like outside of work and try to learn their families. See them as an individual with dreams, goals, strengths, and weaknesses. Overall, view and treat them as your peer – a brother or sister among the human family. And specifically, be genuine.

v. ***Practice:*** Practice does not merely create good; it makes permanent. Once you choose, you want to change – and have the courage to concentrate on this change even though you can't save anything, this means you started practicing. Eventually, your practice can become a habit. Thus, you start your journey to become a great leader.

vi. ***Have Patience and Persevere:*** Once you have determined and vowed to change, enlisting courage, and working on reprogramming yourself with practice, you must next promise never to give up. Have patience because this a method or a process – you may have to deprogram years and even decades of habits – habits of perception, approach, and how you view others. Practices are easy and straightforward for us and take little energy to execute, and we tend to believe in our habit. Thus, you will find yourself upset and feel you must compel to change instantly. You may think that if you were the right person, you would have changed by now. So, do not worry; it typically takes time. If you are honest, genuine, and can work on these steps, you will eventually be victorious over yourself.

Chapter-4

Different types of Stereotypical Leadership

There are mainly two types of stereotypes that leaders present in today's world. One version called gender stereotype, where people know and realized that a female leader could lead the show. Still, being a female, our society typecast them to specific predefined activity, which they have been performing from ages. Females have proved their capability many times, but still, the world has not opened enough to welcome all of them or promote them, the way they do it for male leaders.

Another Version is called stereotype mindset, usually, in gender stereotype, they only target the females, but in this version, sometimes target will not be aware that they are stereotyped. Here the rule is "no rule." Here are some general signs. If you are not fit into someone's mindset, then you can be a target. If you are hurting a leader's ego, knowingly or unknowingly, then you can be a target, and the most common one is, If you have all the potential to become a leader, then you can be a target. This version of stereotype is ruthless and dangerous.

This version will leave the target alone and promotes a person with whom leaders feel comfortable. It is the version where leaders remove their future roadblock or a potential threat according to their creepy mindset, but in general, we destroy a potential leader before someone grows as a full-fledged leader.

In this chapter, I will explain both the types/ version with real-time and life examples.

Chapter-4a: Type-2 Stereotypical Leadership – Gender Stereotype: Does leader gender make the difference?

Kofi Annan, former secretary-general of the united nations, said, "Gender equality is more than a goal. It is a precondition for meeting the challenge of reducing poverty, promoting sustainable development, and building good governance."

Gender is not equivalent to sex. Sex alludes to the organic attributes of people. Interestingly, Gender alludes to socially characterized jobs and practices for people. At the point when we anticipate that people should act with a goal in mind, since they are male and female, at that point, we follow sexual orientation standards.

Various societies can have distinctive gender standards or different ways they anticipate that people should act.

For instance, a few communities predict that ladies should remain at home and do family unit errands, while men ought to go out to work. These standards are likewise called sexual orientation jobs, which are specific jobs people are relied upon to perform inside society or even inside the family.

Gender Stereotype generalizations allude to banalities which a man or lady should do or resemble:

- Women are nurses, not doctors
- Men are doctors, not nurses
- Women are supposed to cook and do housework
- Men are supposed to have a job
- Women are caring and friendly
- Men are though and messy
- Women are followers
- Men are leaders
- Women should look pretty
- Men should be good at sports

Roles and jobs are not gendered specific. Instead, they are found out and forced by social qualities! In any case, everything that a man can do, a woman can do as well, and the other way around!

- ***Gender Identity:*** Individuals can likewise relate to various sexual orientations. A few people may be organically brought into the world a man (=sex, natural), yet feel progressively like a Woman (=gender).

Individuals from all religions, nations, networks, families can distinguish themselves in a variety of ways:

- ○ *Cisgender:* People who distinguish themselves as the gender, with they brought into the world.
- ○ *Transgender:* People who distinguish themselves with a sexual orientation other than the gender, with they brought into the world.
- ○ *Trans-sexual:* People distinguish themselves with a sexual orientation other than the gender, with they brought into the world and have experienced a gender change.

- *Gender Equality:* Gender equality is a fundamental human right and depicted as; "every person brought into the world equivalent." It implies that everybody, regardless of whether born as male, female, or intersex, ought to have the option to build up their maximum capacity and live in opportunity and nobility. Examples of gender equality are.
  - ○ *Equivalent access to education*
  - ○ *Equivalent access to mobility*
  - ○ *Comparable job opportunities and salaries*
  - ○ *Freedom of marrying whom you want*
  - ○ *Equivalent divorce rights*

Two experimental studies analyzed whether gender stereotypes about the transformational, value-based, and free enterprise administration styles comprise a bit of leeway or a hindrance for women's access to leadership positions in organizations.

The initial examination explored the precision of elucidating gender stereotypes about leadership styles, demonstrating that members precisely accept that women show more transformational and unexpected reward behaviors, and fewer management-by-exception and laissez-faire behaviors than men.

The subsequent examination researched prescriptive stereotypes about the significance of leadership styles for the promotion of women and men to various levels in organizations. Helpful inspiration was more significant for men than ladies and particularly significant for development to CEO. Conversely, individualized thought was more notable for women than men and particularly substantial for promotion to senior management.

Consistent with these stereotypical beliefs about Leadership, women keen on promotion might be all around encouraged to mix individualized thought and effective inspiration practices.

Women keep climbing the rungs of power—building their positions as heads of state, corporate leaders, and media influencers—however, their minority status implies they, despite everything, face unforgiving, restricting evaluations dependent on their gender. "Women are being judged more, even by other women," said Valerie Young, Ed.D., author of The Secret Thoughts of Successful Women. While male leaders are permitted to have complex characters, influential women regularly summarized by hackneyed stereotypes that subvert them and their power.

Forbes Woman found a significant number of the world's most influential women, from IMF chief Christine Lagarde to Jill Abramson of the New York Times, to ask: What is your least favorite stereotype about powerful women? Gender and Career specialists additionally said something regarding the perilous thoughts about women's achievement and how they saturate the aggregate inner mind. The following represent the ten most detested and inescapable stereotypes.

- *No. 1: Ice Queen:* Halley Bock, CEO of leadership and development training company Fierce, takes note that the savage "Ice Queen" stereotype is rampant. Cultural delineations, as bone-chilling magazine editor Miranda Priestly in The Devil Wears Prada and manipulating boss Patty Hewes on Damages, paint successful women as unsympathetic power mongers.

It is, obviously, a Catch-22. "A woman who shows feeling in the workplace is frequently cast as too fragile or unstable to lead," Bock said. "A woman who shows no emotion and keeps it hyper-professional is frigid and unfeminine. For some women, it tends to be a hopeless scenario."

- *No. 2: Single and Lonely:* Harvard instructor Olivia Fox Cabane noticed that the positive perception that influential women are intimidating to men and should forfeit their personal lives might prevent women from the following power. Indeed, even those women who aren't keen on marrying, face harsh judgment. Men get the opportunity to be "lone rangers." At the same time, women are diminished to "spinsters" and "old-maid." truth be told, when Janet Napolitano was designated Secretary of Homeland Security, critics said her being single would permit her to "invest more time on the Job."

- *No. 3: Tough:* The first female Executive Editor of The New York Times, Jill Abramson, is not stereotypical. She had a hard-charging career as an investigative reporter at The Wall Street Journal and altered her way to the highest point of the Times masthead. She is additionally a true-blood New Yorker and is writing a book about puppies.

Despite her complexities, she must contend with being designated "tough" and "brusque," making the "she is-tough stereotype" her least favorite. Said Abramson: "As an investigative reporter, I had intense norms and an impressive method of encircling and revealing stories, however, I don't consider myself as a tough person."

- *No. 4: Weak:* Costa Rica President Laura Chinchilla, the country's first female leader, told that successful women face generally typecasting because society is still adjusting to women's' ongoing decision-making power. Chinchilla accepts the most pervasive stereotype is that women are "weak," a perception that may come from women's greater desire to manufacture an accord. "We comprehend success not as the result of only one individual but as a result of a team," she said. The diverse method of managing power often misjudged as a kind of weakness."

- *No. 5: Masculine:* The idea that influential women must be, lead and seem as though a man profoundly disturbs Christine Lagarde, the managing director of the International Monetary Fund. In a video meeting with FORBES, she said, siphoning her clench hand, she abhors the possibility that "you need to look like a businessman."

She admitted that sometimes, she feels the pressure to look the "right" way but tries to resist not being "excessively business-like."

- *No. 6: Conniving:* When NBC's Curry started her career, she told us that she could not be a news reporter because women had "no news judgment." Now, she is at the top of her game and says the stereotype that most affront her is "the idea that a woman can only be successful because they know the tricks of conniving their rise - that a woman could not arise simply because of their talent and they are too good to be denied. She has encountered it herself, saying that she gets asked as to whether she "constrained" NBC to give her the anchor work or if there was a "backroom deal" Curry told that, "I discover it truly irritating."

- *No. 7: Emotional:* Ellen Lubin-Sherman, executive coach and author of business guide The Essentials of Fabulous, believes one the riskiest stereotype female leaders will face is that they are inclined to emotional outbursts. Regardless of Secretary of State Hillary Clinton's steady collected disposition, when she teared up on the campaign trail, the media pounced. Similarly, former Yahoo leader Carol Bartz is frequently referring to for her "salty language," which utilized as proof that she is "emotional" and a "loose cannon."

- *No. 8: Angry:* "Anger is an indication of status in men; however, when ladies show anger, they are being portrayed as less competent," said Young. First Lady Michelle Obama was condemned as an "angry black woman" when she was campaigning for her husband in the 2008 presidential election. The Harvard-trained legal advisor scrupulously softened her image and speeches to look more "amiable," becoming better known for her fashion and her unending support of her husband than for her position on political issues.

- *No. 9: A Token:* Women hold only 16% of corporate board seats. Whereas focusing on balancing things out, the board always undervalue them as a "token" of diversity instead of having earned the post. Former U.S. Secretary of State Condoleezza Rice was often the only woman in the room; however, her gender did not get her there. "When organizations pay attention to their objectives and diversity goals. They won't settle for a less than the best candidate for the job," said Lynne Sarikas, director of the MBA vocation focus at Northeastern University. "women should be hired based on their education, experience, and what they can accomplish for the organization."

- *No. 10: A Cheerleader:* Billie Blair, president, and CEO of Change Strategists, takes note of that noticeable woman who is considered feminine and warmed may be dismissed as "cheerleaders" rather than the strong leader they are. When a former Alaska Governor Sarah Palin was running for VP, Blair was flabbergasted to hear a male client depict her as "a cheerleader, not a mentor/Coach nor a quarterback."

Leaders are often depicted as male, even when we think of a leader and try to draw a picture in our mind; a male figure always comes out as a result. We always ignore the strength and capacity of women. History has proved several times that women are no less as a leader compared to men, but still, they are being treated weaker leader or incompetent leader compared to men.

Chapter-4b: Type-1 Stereotypical Leadership – Being a Leader saving the biased person the trouble of learning

The word stereotype denotes a belief a few bound styles of individual, a bunch of people, or roles that folks match. Whether or not we tend to admit it or maybe understand it, we have got stereotypes for all kinds of individuals and functions.

- In our minds, we tend to place people and roles into silos and category.

- We have expectations of people and roles based on our views rather than who the person might be or what the position is to do.

- We maintain preconceived notions about such people and roles.

- We feel exonerated when people act the way we said they would and surprised when they do not.

Even if we tend to agree that stereotypes are often limiting or maybe hurtful, they exist. What do you think when someone mentions about used car salesman or the politician? What about specific C-suite executives?

It appears that when somebody has not had an experience with a specific stereotype, they inherently realize it or will relate somehow. Stereotypes seem to permeate our lives, and the issue with stereotypes is that they regularly produce barriers and impediments for us. For possible relationships, we would wish to have and can benefit greatly.

While stereotypes would appear negative, they will even have value if we chose to take the required action. If we all know that they exist, then we can prepare ourselves for how we might manage them effectively. We can consider how we would improve them or help them do away with them altogether in our sphere of influence. In different words, the fact that stereotypes exist means we can use that knowledge to introduce change and to search out ways in which to make a difference.

In business, leaders and managers are not exempt from stereotypes. In every organization, there are different types of leaders and managers that we can relate to them. Maybe we tend to have not thought of; however, we would categorize them if we were to certain people we know, we might seemingly realize ourselves agreeing about their behaviors, characteristics, and work style as compared to others.

The challenge and risk with describing any stereotype are that there will be common themes across some or all. The objective here is not to endorse stereotype; however, instead, point out that these fours do exist in every organization and are the ones all of us would have experienced and have had our colleagues often describing them. Those fours are the doer, the fixer, the maker, and the suit. Here are some pros and cons of these four categories.

The Doer
Pros

- Hands-on, gets stuff done, and desires to check tangible results.
- Tends to lead by example, is not afraid to dig deep and get involved.
- Strong work ethic seldom thinks or says, "it's not my job."

Cons

- Sometimes too hand-on gets in the way of others who should be leading
- Can lean towards micromanagement, not trusting of the group or organization
- Typically, has too much on their plate, believe they must have a hand in everything.

The Fixer

Pros

- Go to the person when a resolution requires for any problem, sometimes includes a sensible answer.
- Leverages their network well – appears to know and recognize everybody – "I know a guy."
- They are known as being handy, providing creative solutions to most issues and challenges.

Cons

- It can be over-confident in their ability to "fix" things and getting stretched thin.
- It does not merely admit they could not have the solution in fear of losing the respect and trust of peers and direct reports.
- Exaggeration generally makes up for insecurity – it is not uncommon for them to perpetually have a story or share a related experience that makes them look good in front of others.

The Maker
Pros

- Oozes with expertise and credibility, proven in their respective field
- Typically, well-liked and respected, charismatic, and trusted by colleagues.
- The Good manager is always aware of the ways to hold the team together.

Cons

- They can believe their press clippings, making them ineffective and arrogant.
- Past success will result in losing focus in the here and now, in other words forgetting that you just cannot live off of yesterday's breakfast.
- There is a risk of losing the mental toughness required to keep moving things in the right direction.

The Suit
Pros

- It can be a good figurehead for the given based on their past success and history.
- Possesses credibility though they do not have specific business expertise.
- They tend to be an excellent networker and social butterfly.

Cons

- They seem to take credit for all good things, no matter how small they are.
- They always look out for themselves than others, and they are usually selfish by nature.
- Sometimes a touch sterile with their approaching style and the way they work – not looking to get their hands dirty, delegation serves as a substitute for only not willing to get involved.

In the end, our aim regardless of what role we play ought to be to avoid the lure of stereotypes, and our focus should be on how we can leverage what people in our organization do best so that we are all fit for purpose.

In the words of Colin Powell, a National Leader, "Fit no stereotypes. Do not chase the latest management fads. The situation dictates which approach best accomplishes the team's mission".

Examples of Stereotypical Mindset:

Now I will narrate two of the recent experiences of one of my Friend "Sakshi," which will give a fair idea of a stereotypical mindset and how they can be dangerous with times.

Sakshi was stereotyped several times in her last organization. The story began in somewhere in the middle of 2019. Sakshi had a new Managing Director joined by Jul-Aug-2019. The new MD had made it clear and loud in the first townhall meet when he said the following "If this is supposed to be a jungle, then I am the only Lion here." It not only replicates the personality of the new MD but also sends an alarm to the Sr. Leaders but sadly, which was ignored by all, and everyone assumes that the MD has told this humorously, but no one pays attention towards the tone and tenor of the dialogue.

Soon after this, the story began, as the new MD had a generous struggle in understanding the technology, platforms, and culture of the organizations. So, it was apparent that things started to fall apart strategically. The failure increased the pressure and changed the entire office atmosphere altogether, which had started hitting the new MD hard. Since then, he started targeting the groups who will not align with him and who are not ready to take the accountability of the strategical failure.

The Best case scenario is to do a failure analysis and to understand the root cause of the failure, instead of that the MD started supporting and backing up the teams who provide their unconditional support to him, despite the reason, those teams might be the cause for the epic strategic failure.

It was like a condition where two of the group supporting each other for their survival, whereas they realized and knew that their sustainability chances are zero.

Then the time came, when the MD and all the groups associated with MD, started targeting the technology group/practice director, where Sakshi was working. They also had figured out that Sakshi being the most natural target, as she was working as a project leader, and in most of the companies, the project leader will not have a business dependency. So, they started plotting and framing up stories. Here are the processes of how Sakshi falls into their trap.

- *Conflict with Operations/ Recruitment team*

  Sakshi had an average performing contractor in her team. All of a sudden, the operations team start showing interest in removing the same contractor stating non-performance. Sakshi immediately resisted this and condemned them, saying it's delivery team call to decide whom to let go and with whom they will continue. Which, in return, hit the operations team extremely hard, and they started highlighting this to Sr. Leaders. In the end, the operations team succeed to remove the contractor.

That is when the real challenge came, as the resource was billing to the client and was generating revenue for the organization, so Sakshi asked for immediate backup, which the recruitment and operations team took eight months to backfill. During these eight months, Sakshi was replicating the billing losses to her Sr. Leaders, which again was hitting hard to the recruitment and the operations team.

In this case, the local recruitment & operations leaders teamed up with the MD and tried to convince the Sr. Leaders that Sakshi is not capable in some way or other. They even tried to portray a negative picture of Sakshi and her technology group.

- Sakshi followed the best practices and processes, which anyone else could also have done.
- Sakshi had informed the operations/ recruitment team that, as per the process, it's a delivery team responsibility and accountability to add or remove resources.
- Sakshi highlighted the revenue losses due to the sudden removal of the resource with operations intervention.

Here, in this case, the Stereotypical mindset comes into the picture, where the operations leaders and MD cannot be able to bear that a person-way lower than their designation is advising them the processes and best practices. It should always be either their way or no way.

- *Conflict with Internal shared-services (QA) team*

   Sakshi's Organization had a new QA manager onboarded in the month of Sep-2019, the QA manager shows the real intention right at the beginning. Ideally, when someone joins a company as a manager, they try to understand current as-is processes, best practices, policy, and company culture. Then if they find any loopholes, they can put across their suggestion for improvisation.

   But the QA manager tried to enforce her policy, processes, and best practices.

   Soon the entire QA team started feeling the wrath due to a series of restrictions, policies, and processes to follow, which put them under tremendous pressure. Some of the QA resources tried to complain to Sr. Leaders, but nothing worked as the new QA manager was getting complete support from the Operations leaders and the MD.

Soon this entire process started impacting Sakshi's technology group and all the subsequent projects. As per the company policy, there is only a limited work from home allowed in a month, whereas Sakshi used to approve more than the set limit due to some exceptional cases and some business-critical cases. In Jan- 2020, Sakshi had a new project kicked-off, and the project was in the discovery phase, which requires much effort from resources, and even there were some late-night calls, which enforces all the project resources to connect from home most of the time. Which was approved by Sakshi, being a primary approving authority?

At the same time, the QA manager had asked all QA resources to take leave, as they had availed their set limit of work from home for the month. It leaves the entire project at risk, so being a project leader, Sakshi escalated this to the Sr. Leaders, Project Leaders, and the local leaders, including the MD, with an expectation that this will get a proper resolution.

Simultaneously the other hand, the QA manager raised a complaint to QA director, technology head, and the MD that Sakshi is micro-managing and not allowing resources to connect from home even though they have late-night meetings.

She also added that Sakshi is threatening to all her resources that if they go against her, then their annual reviews will be impacted. It all happening in the background, and Sakshi was not aware of these complaints until the beginning of Mar-2020.

The QA director and the technology head based out of the US, and both of them hired the QA manager, so they will support the resources they have recruited. On the other hand, the India MD always have his support for the QA manager. All of them form allies which include, QA Manager, QA Director, Technology Head, India MD, Operations Director, and HR Manager. They were performing investigations on the background to substantiate the allegation raised by the QA manager. Still, to Sakshi's surprise, she had not been informed anything about this and not even included in the investigations.

She was expecting a solution to her initial escalation to Sr. leader, which never resolved. Still, in return, as an outcome of the coveted investigation, they come up with a solution to remove Sakshi as it is impacting the company culture and values.

When Sakshi asked what kind of investigations it was and why she wasn't informed about the same, then the answer is what surprised her a lot, and the answer was, "we were instructed by Sr. Leaders not to inform you anything."

She tried doing counterargument as every other human would also have done the same. She even told how an investigation could perform without involving both the parties, i.e., the one who raised the complaint and the other one who is accused of having the fault. But nothing worked, and She had to accept and leave.

- o Sakshi followed the process and best practices, like every other project leader, her primary focus was on project delivery and customer satisfaction which she did it somewhat.
- o Sakshi did not ever force any resources to come to the office; as a human and a woman, she completely understands that they had lots of pressure from the work point of view.

The way things are executed is the traditional way of any situation of project delivery. Still, it hurt the QA manager the most that, her resource and her team may not respect the way they are admiring the project leader.

The only reason was that Sakshi was giving more space to all her resources.

Lastly, the investigation was done only within the QA director, Technology head, MD, Operations Director, HR Manager, and QA manager. It clearly shows that they have considered Sakshi as a threat, and they are sure that Sakshi may end up their traditional way of leading people, so they removed Sakshi.

In both instances, leaders were feeling insecure. The same insecurity leads to the flourishing of their ego's to the next level, where they can't think of any profit or loss, they only focus on their ego's, and they nurture it to come out as the winner. Still, in reality, they are at the losing end, which they may not realize it now. In another way, stereotypical leadership always pushes you to save your favorite.

Stereotypical Leadership will affect the individual, and in the longer-term, it will affect the organizations. Organizations may lose some of their best resources, and it will impact the organization's reputation in the global market and platform like LinkedIn, Glassdoor, Instahyre, and many such platforms.

Chapter-5

Good Leader v/s Stereotypic Leaders

A Stereotypical leader is a boss; you despise working for every day; the one who never acknowledges your achievement and only emphasizes your fault. Even though they recognize your performance, that must be associated with some benefits in return for them.

Whereas a good leader will be a selfless personality and honestly believes in the work they do, and their team does. They have a strong sense of purpose that materializes in even the most menial tasks. They acknowledge all their team member's achievements and always encourage them.

How do we differentiate a good leader and a stereotypical leader? What difference do they create?

It is an important question that every leader must ask themselves. Each leader faces difficulties and situations every day that test their patience, skills, attitude, and mindset. There is no magical, drama-free team, what differentiates a good leader v/s Stereotypical leader is how they handle the challenges and situations they face every day.

I will explain with five situations that are handled very differently by leaders based on their good and bad approaches. Hop this case study will help everyone to improve as a leader.

Before we move on to the case studies, I would like to share a picture, which will help you to differentiate an excellent and Stereotypical leader.

- *Good leader v/s. Stereotypical leader: A employee's idea*

The Situation: An employee comes to you with a suggestion or an idea to help the team. As a leader, it is something that you probably have done and already taken care of it but have not gotten around.

Approach: -1 – Being a Stereotypical Leader:

Stereotypical Leader: While they might not have intended to, it feels very annoying that they are trying to tell me what needs to be done. I am either going to overlook what they said or come up with a few reasons not to figure out something to blister them.

The Result: Your team will get the hang of putting forth proposals does not worth the effort. Much will go unsaid; a good idea will lay torpid, and your team is likely to complain about you behind your back, or they may even start mocking you behind your back.

Approach-2 – Being a Good/ Genuine Leader:

Good/ Genuine Leader: It is no way fun to face harsh truths, but you embrace it. You perceive that your team needs to feel comfortable carrying their concerns, ideas, and thoughts to you, so you express gratitude for their feedback. You additionally pose a couple of inquiries to be sure you comprehend their recommendation completely.

The Result: Your team member feels heard, and you increase a new understanding of why you might need to knock an issue or opportunity up your priority list.

Feedback from your team is an opportunity and a lifeline for good leaders; they see so much you do not get the chance to give all your responsibilities.

- ***Good leader v/s. Stereotypical leader: Questions from your team***

  The Situation: An employee in a long meeting asks a tough question: they zoom out and question the value of the project, which is being the primary focus in the team. "How did we get here? What made us decide to do this in the first place?"

Approach: -1 – Being a Stereotypical Leader:

Stereotypical Leader: You feel shocked and offended, you think of yourself, that "how dare they question my decision?" You glare at your team and change the subject to focus back on the original discussion. Sometimes to avoid their question, leaders usually respond, saying it has been a decision taken by Sr. Leadership, whereas you are very well aware of how this is prioritized.

The Result: A chilling effect clears over your team. Your team is very well aware, not to bring up or raise tough questions to you in a group meeting and simply oblige things. Group debate is an expression, which is unfamiliar to your team.

Approach-2 – Being a Good/ Genuine Leader:

Good/ Genuine Leader: You take a deep breath and address the question head-on. Contingent upon the circumstance, you either explain the inspirations for the decision they may not know for the benefit of the whole team, or you connect with them Socratically to allow questions to them to uncover the reasoning.

If the way they asked was disruptive, you converse with them about it in their next 1-1 or privately after the meeting.

The Result: Your team sees that with you, there are no imbecilic questions, and it is safe to stir things up. It enables your group to investigate new thoughts or ideas thoroughly and avoid missing the forest for the trees.

It tends to be challenging to oversee individuals who have strong opinions and ideas, yet they can likewise be your most prominent resource. If you remember that you are all on the same team and trying to win together, you can abstain from feeling cynical about their remarks.

The best part is that if you work on your skills and ability to ask questions, you can connect with them and your entire team to have a deep understanding of where they are coming from and the best solution going forward.

- *Good leader v/s. Stereotypical leader: Managing the unknown*

The Situation: You have someone on your team in a role you have never done yourself. You are curious about all the subtlety of what precisely the role is all about, and you are not sure the key to success for the same function.

Approach: -1 – Being a Stereotypical Leader:

Stereotypical Leader: You feel a bit threatened by the recruit, and some imposter syndrome, so you counterfeit it. You pretend that you know more than you do and go super hands-off with them. They must mention to you what you must know, isn't that so?

The Result: Communication rapidly breaks down between you and the team members. They feign exacerbation when you imagine you know what they are talking about, and Your relationship becomes antagonistic as your team tries to manage you out of the way so they can simply complete their work.

Approach-2 – Being a Good/ Genuine Leader:

Good/ Genuine Leader: Recognizing your knowledge gap, you take it head-on. You invest your time with your team to learn from them and ask questions politely when you don't understand something, Together, you come up with a plan where you can hold your team accountable for the work you are less familiar.

The Result: You will able to build more trust with them and show that your team has a culture of quietude for things they do not know. By having a plan, you can still tell how they are performing relative to expectations despite your relative newness to their field of work.

As significant as building up the task-relevant maturity for your team is, your task-relevant maturity matters, too. Grasping the need to learn new abilities and concede when you do not know is a growth mindset attitude, and it is well worth demonstrating.

- ***Good leader v/s. Stereotypical leader: Working with different personalities and cultures***

The Situation: Your organization is dabbling in remote work or recruiting from outside your region. You were raised in an area where everyone says things indirectly and gently, but your new hire is more direct than others.

Approach: -1 – Being a Stereotypical Leader:

Stereotypical Leader: Resentful of their communication style, you censure them for all communication issues. After all, you are the boss, so they should adopt the form of the process that you follow, or you like the most. Using your suitable style, you drop unpretentious clues that they appear to be disregarding, causing you a deep sense of dissatisfaction for you.

The Result: You both become progressively disappointed with each other. You feel like your team members are abrasive, and they feel like they cannot able to get a straight answer from you. It makes you both need to dodge the other, prompting poor teamwork.

Approach-2 – Being a Good/ Genuine Leader:

Good/ Genuine Leader: Perceiving their distinction in character, you put forth an effort to understand them better. You try to be more explicit in your communication with them, and not flinch an excess of when they are more straightforward than you. You additionally mentor them on the most proficient method to get the point across with somewhat smoother edges.

The Result: While it is difficult, you work together to arrive at a comprehension by the way you both communicate with each other. Finding the common grounds leads to a better outcome, and open communication keeps ideas streaming between you both.

Whenever there is a problem with your team, it is essential to start by looking in the mirror. There is continually something you were doing (or not doing) to add to the issue. A healthy dose of self-awareness can assist you in starting from how you can do your part to improve difficult situations. The best part is that when you lead the way by taking all the problems head-on, you make it simpler for your team to admit and accept their faults and do best in their part as well.

- *Good leader v/s. Stereotypical leader: Rolling up your sleeves*

The Situation: You take the help of a coach to be a better leader. The coach tells you passionately you must do something which you are not used to before.

Approach: -1 – Being a Stereotypical Leader:

Stereotypical Leader: You disregard the guidance, thinking, "It's additional work, and I'm certain it can wait for some more time. I don't see them for a month in any case." You let your mind flee why the guidance does not have any significant bearing or is not as significant as the 38 different things on your plan for the day.

The Result: You pass up the effect your coach realized the exertion could have. Intensifying the issue, when they see you haven't rolled out the improvement, they begin to lose confidence in your ability to tune in. Soon, they are less interested in coaching you or stay away from specific topics that could help, however, appear to fail to be noticed by you.

Approach-2 – Being a Good/ Genuine Leader:

Good/ Genuine Leader: You perceive that you picked this coach for their experience and insights. If they are passionate about doing this now, it must be significant. It is not easy making time, yet you discover approaches to carve out enough to complete it on priority alongside your regular tasks and activities.

The Result: You complete the exertion, and you perceive how it begins to affect your team in manners you never anticipated. Your coach additionally turns out to be progressively positive about working with you, seeing that it is a good investment of their time. They proceed to challenge and push you to turn out to be a better result of it.

There will never be sufficient hours in the day to do all that we would like to do. That is the reason it's so critical to deal with your schedule well, so you don't fill it just with low-value tasks. Regardless of whether you decide to eat the frog before anything else, or utilize the stones, sand, and water analogy to spending plan your time, making a point to complete the essential things which are critical to your success and growth as a leader.

Sometimes things can be hard because of multiple things running in parallel. The distinction between a Good leader v/s a Stereotypical leader is frequently subtle. It is everything in your mindset and your ability to take ownership and responsibility of problems and opportunities in a positive manner.

Chapter-6

Summary & Conclusion

Summary:

while a Stereotypical leader may also showcase these all the qualities to various ranges, I have mentioned in Chapter-2. All proper leaders leverage at least a few —or most — of the mentioned traits. Collectively, they make up the spine of leadership throughout leader stages, industries, and continents. Without these skills, proper management is impossible.

In case you do not sense like those traits of an incredibly good leader appropriately describe you, do not panic — there are approaches to improve in your leadership skills. We all know and accept it as real that leaders are not born but made. We understand that leaders are molded through experience, persevered, look at, and adapt. In other words, you may fortify any of the characteristics and traits of an excellent leader in case you are open to growth and also you positioned within the effort and time in the direction of self-improvement. Moreover, organizations can help their resources hone these talents via leadership development training and actual-global revel.

It is also crucial to comprehend that leadership is a social system. Leadership is not a vacation spot — it is something that you will have to learn frequently for the duration of your career, no matter what level you attain in an organization.

Leadership is less about A robust or charismatic individual and more approximately a group of people running together to acquire effects. That is why we say that leadership is a journey — distinctive groups, tasks, conditions, and organizations would require you to use those capabilities in distinct approaches.

Usually, Leadership consists of three elements: direction, alignment, and commitment. in case you demonstrate several of the traits of a good leader, however, fail to grasp this, probabilities are like you will get far on your own with your struggle and self-learning. You will be well-favored and respected; however, it will be tough to perform team or organizational goals without a settlement on targets, coordination to meet them, and a dedication to creating it takes place.

Organizations can foster deeper tiers of leadership at work through an expansion of development possibilities ranging from on-the-process learning to an offsite leadership improvement software. However, individuals should not wait to begin strengthening the leadership quality and characteristics of a remarkable leader inside themselves.

Conclusion:

To join the elite club of desirable leaders, you ought to have a lot of these features, but if you lack a number of those features, then you can fill the gaps with self-development and with the change in your mindset. You will have to set a good instance for others to comply with it. That is where your dedication, passion, empathy, honesty, and integrity come into play. Right communication abilities and choice-making talents also play a critical function in the fulfillment and failure of a pacesetter. Lastly, innovation, and creative thinking, in addition to the futuristic vision, are a couple of leadership qualities that make up a person to be a good leader.

Reference:

Gwendolyn L.Gerber 1988 | *Article on Leadership roles and the gender stereotype traits Article*

Alex Adamopoulos 2018 | *Article on Leadership Stereotypes | Article published by emergn*

Mark Graybill 2016 | *Article on Stereotyping is Bad Leadership | Article published in About Leaders*

Valerie Petit 2014 | *Article on Male stereotype of a leader persists | Article published in Financial Times*

Claartje J. Vinkenburg, Marloes L.van Engen, Alice H.Eagly, Mary C.Johannesen-Schmidt 2011 | *Article on An exploration of stereotypical beliefs about leadership styles: Is transformational leadership a route to women's promotion? | Article Published in Science Direct*

Sarah E. Saint-Michel 2018 | *Article on Leader gender stereotypes and transformational leadership: Does leader sex make the difference? | Article published in cairn.info*

Julie Warnez 2018 | *Article on (Wo)men in leadership — breaking down the gender stereotypes | Article published in Hudson*

Gregory Lewis 2017 | *Article on 3 Traits of Effective Leaders That Will Shatter Your Stereotypes* | *Articles published in LinkedIn*

Sarmad Hasan 2019 | *Article on Top 15 Leadership Qualities That Make Good Leaders.* | *Article published by blog.tasque.com*

Adam Enfroy 2020 | *Article on 11 Leadership Qualities: A List of Skills to Make a Good Leader.* | *Article published in his website adamenfroy.com*

ccl.org blog 2020 | *Article on What Are the Characteristics of a Good Leader?*

getlighthouse.com 2018 | *Article on Good Leader vs. Bad Leader: 5 Situations You Face Every Day*

Shelby Graves 2018 | *Article on How the Workplace Adopts Stereotypical Male Leadership Roles* | *Article published in digitalcommons.liu.edu*

About the Author

Abhishek Mishra aims to create a new platform or forum to facilitate discussion when people or leaders feel they are stuck and confused or unable to add value. He wanted to help and create a platform where people help and support each other, where there is no gender differentiation and where people become role models for each other.

As a writer, he has accomplished and accolades for his ability to express his feelings through his words. He has written a few articles which were liked by many professionals over platforms like LinkedIn.

When he is not writing books, you can find him doing project management, and when he is not doing either of these, then you can find him baking awesome cakes. Oh, man! It would be best if you tried his cakes and pastries. He is the kind of person who has loads of energy and does not like to sit idle.

His first book — "The Book of Powerful & Exceptional Quotes — hits the shelves and internet on 26th May-2020. The book is a personal collection of quotes and all the quotes based on Abhishek's life experiences.

He has got stunning writing skills, Culinary skills, and strong management skills, not just that he is also a process-oriented person. In a way, he always keeps trying different things, and this shows his inquisitive nature too.

Professionally he is a project manager, so he has been associated with multiple non-profitable groups to learn and discover ways to help the community and society. You can connect with him at https://www.linkedin.com/in/abhishek-author/. He would love to connect and expand his knowledge sphere.

Apart from writing and project management, Abhishek provides services in ghost-writing, Resume writing, and ghost editing services on demand. His writing skills may be confirmed independently through his books.

For queries & questions related to the book and for any collaboration, please write to him at authorabhishek1206@gmail.com.